2

14

30

Tu Traditional Quilts

Six designs by Nancy Rink feature a mix of traditional patchwork and appliqué techniques. They range in size from wall hangings and throws to bed quilts.

LEISURE ARTS, INC. • Maumelle, Arkansas

Cake Stand

Finished Quilt Size: 47" x 55½" (119 cm x 141 cm)
Finished Block Size: 6" x 6" (13 cm x 13 cm)

SHOPPING LIST

*Yardage is based on 43"/44" (109 cm/112 cm)
wide fabric with a usable width of 40" (102 cm).*

- ☐ ⅝ yd (57 cm) of slate blue fabric (inner borders and blocks)
- ☐ ½ yd (46 cm) of teal fabric (binding and blocks)
- ☐ ⅜ yd (34 cm) *each* of 2 assorted medium to dark blue fabrics (blocks)
- ☐ 1⅜ yds (1.7 m) of putty fabric (outer borders and blocks)
- ☐ 1⅜ yds (1.7 m) of beige fabric (alternate blocks, setting triangles, and blocks)
- ☐ ⅜ yd (34 m) *each* of 3 assorted cream and tan fabrics (blocks)
- ☐ 2¾ yds (2.5 m) of backing fabric
- ☐ 55" x 64" (140 cm x 163 cm) piece of batting

CUTTING THE PIECES

*Follow **Rotary Cutting**, page 34, to cut fabric. Cut all strips from the selvage-to-selvage width of the fabric unless otherwise stated. Borders are cut exact length. All measurements include ¼" seam allowances.*

From slate fabric:
- Cut 2 *lengthwise* side inner borders 2" x 42⅞".
- Cut 2 *lengthwise* top/bottom inner borders 2" x 37⅜".
- Cut 6 **binding strips** 2¼" wide.

From beige fabric:
- Cut 2 strips 6½" wide. From these strips, cut 12 **squares E** 6½" x 6½".
- Cut 1 strip 9¾" wide. From this strip, cut 4 squares 9¾" x 9¾". Cut each square *twice* diagonally to make 16 **side setting triangles F**.
- Cut 1 strip 5⅛" wide. From this strip, cut 2 squares 5⅛" x 5⅛". Cut each square *once* diagonally to make 4 **corner setting triangles G**.

From putty fabric:
- Cut 2 *lengthwise* side outer borders 5½" x 45⅞".
- Cut 2 *lengthwise* top/bottom outer borders 5½" x 47⅜".

From slate blue, teal, assorted blues, beige, putty, tan, and cream fabrics:
- Cut 20 *sets* of the following for the *block background*:
  - Cut 1 **square A** 2" x 2".
  - Cut 2 squares 2⅜" x 2⅜". Cut each square *once* diagonally to make 4 **triangles B**.
  - Cut 2 **rectangles C** 2" x 3½".
  - Cut 1 square 3⅞" x 3⅞". Cut square *once* diagonally to make 2 **triangles D**.
- Cut 20 *sets* of the following for the *cake stand*:
  - Cut 3 squares 2⅜" x 2⅜". Cut each square *once* diagonally to make 6 **triangles B**.
  - Cut 1 square 3⅞" x 3⅞". Cut square *once* diagonally to make 2 **triangles D**.

MAKING THE BLOCKS

*Follow **Piecing** and **Pressing**, page 35, to make the quilt top. Use a ¼" seam allowance throughout.*

1. Sew 1 background **triangle (B)** and 1 cake stand **triangle (B)** together to make **Unit 1**. Make 4 Unit 1's. Press the seam allowance toward the background fabric.

Unit 1(make 4)

2. Sew 1 background **triangle (D)** and 1 cake stand **triangle (D)** together to make **Unit 2**. Press the seam allowance toward the background fabric.

Unit 2

3. Sew 1 **rectangle (C)** and 1 cake stand **triangle (B)** together to make **Unit 3**. Make 1 Unit 3 and 1 Unit 3 reversed.

Unit 3 (make 1 and 1 reversed)

4. Sew 2 **Unit 1's** and 1 background **square (A)** together to make **Unit 4**. Make 2 Unit 4's.

Unit 4 (make 2)

5. Sew 2 **Unit 1's** and 1 **Unit 2** together to make **Unit 5**. Press the seam allowance toward Unit 2.

Unit 5

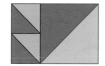

6. Sew **Unit 4** and **Unit 5** together to make **Unit 6**.

Unit 6

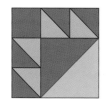

7. Sew Unit 3 and Unit 3 reversed to Unit 6 to make **Unit 7**.

Unit 7

8. Sew 1 **triangle (D)** to **Unit 7** to make the **Block**. Press the seam allowance toward triangle (D).

Block

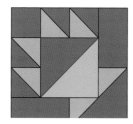

9. Repeat Steps 1-8 to make 20 Blocks.

ASSEMBLING THE QUILT TOP

*Refer to the **Assembly Diagram** to assemble the quilt top.*

1. Lay out Blocks alternately with **squares (E)**, **side setting triangles (F)**, and **corner setting triangles (G)**.
2. Sew **Blocks**, **squares (E)**, and **side setting triangles (F)** together in diagonal **Rows**. Press seam allowances away from Blocks.
3. Sew Rows together. Sew **corner setting triangles (G)** to corners of quilt top.
4. Sew the **side inner borders**, then the **top/bottom inner borders** to the quilt top.
5. Sew the **side outer borders**, then the **top/bottom outer borders** to the quilt top.

Assembly Diagram

COMPLETING THE QUILT

1. Follow **Quilting**, page 38, to mark, layer, and quilt as desired. Quilt shown is quilted with feather motifs in the background and borders and outline quilting in the Blocks.
2. Follow **Making a Hanging Sleeve**, page 41, if a hanging sleeve is desired.
3. Use **binding strips** and follow **Binding**, page 41, to bind quilt.

Glory Days

Finished Quilt Size: 88" x 88" (224 cm x 224 cm)
Finished Block Size: 16" x 16" (41 cm x 41 cm)

SHOPPING LIST

Yardage is based on 43"/44" (109 cm/112 cm) wide fabric with a usable width of 40" (102 cm). Fat quarters are approximately 22" x 18" (56 cm x 46 cm).

- ☐ 1 fat quarter of red and cream paisley print fabric for appliqués
- ☐ 1 fat quarter of light blue print fabric for appliqués
- ☐ ³/₄ yd (69 cm) of blue cable stripe fabric for appliqué vine
- ☐ ¹/₂ yd (46 cm) of blue and cream paisley print fabric for blocks and appliqués
- ☐ ¹/₂ yd (46 cm) of blue and cream plaid print fabric for blocks and appliqués
- ☐ ⁵/₈ yd (57 cm) of navy paisley print fabric for blocks and appliqués
- ☐ ³/₄ yd (69 cm) of pink print fabric for blocks and appliqués
- ☐ 1³/₈ yds (1.3 m) of red cable stripe fabric for appliqués and binding
- ☐ 1¹/₄ yds (1.1 m) of red and pink print fabric for blocks and appliqués
- ☐ 1³/₈ yds (1.3 m) of dark red print fabric for blocks and borders
- ☐ 1¹/₂ yds (1.4 m) of navy print fabric for blocks and borders
- ☐ 4³/₄ yds (4.3 m) of cream and red print fabric for background
- ☐ 8 yds (7.3 m) of fabric for backing
- ☐ freezer paper - 1 strip 10" x 82"
- ☐ template plastic for Needle-Turn Applique´**or** paper-backed fusible web for Machine Appliqué
- ☐ ¹/₂" (12 mm) bias press bar
- ☐ 96" x 96" (244 cm x 244 cm) piece of batting

CUTTING THE PIECES

*Follow **Rotary Cutting**, page 34, to cut fabric. Cut all strips from the selvage-to-selvage width of the fabric. Cut strips from fat quarters parallel to the long edge. The borders are cut longer than needed and will be trimmed to fit quilt top center. All measurements include $1/4$" seam allowances.*

From blue and cream paisley print fabric:
- Cut 3 strips $2^1/_2$" wide. From these strips, cut 32 **squares A** $2^1/_2$" x $2^1/_2$".

From blue and cream plaid print fabric:
- Cut 5 strips $2^1/_2$" wide. From these strips, cut 72 **squares A** $2^1/_2$" x $2^1/_2$".

From navy paisley print fabric:
- Cut 2 strips $4^1/_2$" wide. From these strips, cut 13 **squares C** $4^1/_2$" x $4^1/_2$".
- Cut 2 strips $2^1/_2$" wide. From these strips, cut 48 **squares A** $2^1/_2$" x $2^1/_2$".

From pink print fabric:
- Cut 6 strips $2^7/_8$" wide. From these strips, cut 72 squares $2^7/_8$" x $2^7/_8$". Cut each square in half *once* diagonally to make 144 **triangles B**.

From red cable stripe fabric:
- Cut **square for bias vine** 24" x 24".
- Cut 9 **binding strips** $2^1/_4$" wide.

From red and pink print fabric:
- Cut 8 strips $2^1/_2$" wide. From these strips, cut 120 **squares A** $2^1/_2$" x $2^1/_2$".
- Cut 2 strips $4^1/_2$" wide. From these strips, cut 12 **squares C** $4^1/_2$" x $4^1/_2$".
- Cut 1 strip $3^1/_2$" wide. From this strip, cut 4 **squares F** $3^1/_2$" x $3^1/_2$".

From dark red print fabric:
- Cut 8 strips $2^1/_2$" wide. From these strips, cut 120 **squares A** $2^1/_2$" x $2^1/_2$".
- Cut 6 **inner border strips** $3^1/_2$" wide.

From navy print fabric:
- Cut 5 strips $2^1/_2$" wide. From these strips, cut 72 **squares A** $2^1/_2$" x $2^1/_2$".
- Cut 8 **outer border strips** $3^1/_2$" wide.
- Cut 1 strip $3^1/_2$" wide. From this strip, cut 4 **squares F** $3^1/_2$" x $3^1/_2$".

From cream and red print fabric:
- Cut 4 *lengthwise* borders $10^1/_2$" x $83^1/_2$".
- Cut 7 strips $2^1/_2$" wide. From this strip, cut 60 **rectangles D** $2^1/_2$" x $4^1/_2$".
- Cut 7 strips $4^1/_2$" wide. From these strips, cut 60 **squares C** $4^1/_2$" x $4^1/_2$".
- Cut 5 strips $4^7/_8$" wide. From these strips, cut 36 squares $4^7/_8$" x $4^7/_8$". Cut each square in half *once* diagonally to make 72 **triangles E**.

CUTTING THE APPLIQUÉS

*You can hand or machine appliqué the vine, flowers and leaves. Use patterns, page 44, and follow **Making and Using Templates**, page 36, for hand appliqué **or** follow **Preparing Fusible Appliqués**, page 37, for machine appliqué .*

From red and cream paisley print fabric:
- Cut 4 **flower centers**.
- Cut 16 **leaves**.

From light blue print fabric:
- Cut 16 **leaves**.

From blue cable stripe fabric:
- Cut **square for bias vine** 23" x 23".
- Cut 5 **leaves**.

From blue and cream paisley print fabric:
- Cut 8 **flower centers**.
- Cut 16 **leaves**.

From blue and cream plaid print fabric:
- Cut 15 **leaves**.

From navy paisley print fabric:
- Cut 4 **flowers**.

From pink print fabric:
- Cut 14 **leaves**.

From red cable stripe fabric:
- Cut **rectangle for bias vine** 13" x 31".
- Cut 7 **leaves**.

From red and pink print fabric:
- Cut 8 **flowers**.
- Cut 9 **leaves**.

MAKING THE BLOCKS

*Follow **Piecing** and **Pressing**, page 35, to make the quilt top. Use ¹/₄" seam allowances throughout.*

1. Referring to **Fig. 1** and pressing the seam allowances toward the pink triangles, sew 2 blue & cream plaid **square A's,** 4 pink triangle B's, and 1 blue and cream paisley **square A** together to make **Unit 1**. Make a total of 36. Press the seam allowances toward the pink triangles.

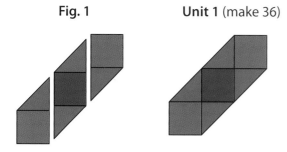

Fig. 1   **Unit 1** (make 36)

2. Finger press 2 cream and red **triangles E** in the center of the long side to mark the center. Matching the centers, sew 1 triangle E to opposite sides of Unit 1 to make **Unit 2**. Press the seam allowances toward the triangles E. Make a total of 36.

Unit 2 (make 36)

3. Draw a diagonal line on the wrong side of each red and pink **square A** and each navy square A. Place 1 red and pink square A on 1 corner of a cream and red **square C.** Stitch on the drawn line (**Fig. 2**). Trim seam allowance to ¹/₄" (**Fig. 3**) and press open.

Fig. 2   **Fig. 3**

In the same manner, add another red and pink **square A** to 1 adjacent corner, then add a navy square A to each remaining corner (**Fig. 4**) to make **Unit 3**. Make 36 Unit 3's.

Fig. 4   **Unit 3** (make 36)

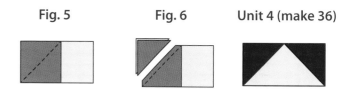

4. Draw a diagonal line on the wrong side of 72 dark red squares A. Place 1 dark red square A on 1 corner of a cream and red **rectangle D**. Stitch on the drawn line (**Fig. 5**). trim seam allowance to ¹/₄" (**Fig. 6**) and press open. Repeat with another dark red square A on opposite corner to make **Unit 4**. Make 36 Unit 4's.

Fig. 5   **Fig. 6**   **Unit 4 (make 36)**

5. Sew 1 Unit 3 and 1 Unit 4 together to make **Unit 5**. Press the seam allowances toward the Unit 2. Make 36 Unit 5's.

Unit 5 (make 36)

6. Pressing seam allowances in directions indicated by arrows, sew 4 Unit 1's, 4 Unit 5's, and 1 navy **square C** into rows. Sew rows together to make a **Block**. Make 9 Blocks.

Block (make 9)

MAKING THE SASHINGS

1. Using the same construction method that you used to construct a Unit 3, use 48 red and pink squares A, 48 dark red squares A, and 24 cream and red squares C to make 24 **Unit 6's**.

Unit 6 (make 24)

2. Using the same construction method that you used to construct a Unit 4, use 48 navy squares A and 24 cream and red rectangles D to make 24 **Unit 7's**.

Unit 7 (make 24)

3. Sew 1 Unit 6 and 1 Unit 7 together to make **Unit 8**. Press the seam allowances toward the Unit 5. Make a total of 36 Unit 7's.

Unit 8 (make 36)

4. Sew 2 Unit 8's and 1 red and pink **square C** together to make a **Sashing**. Make 12 Sashings.

Sashing (make 12)

ASSEMBLING THE QUILT TOP

*Refer to **Quilt Top Center Diagram**, page 12, to assemble the quilt top center.*

1. Sew 3 Blocks and 2 sashings together to make a **block row**. Make 3 block rows.

2. Sew 3 Blocks and 2 navy paisley squares together to make a **sashing row**. Make 2 sashing rows.

3. Sew Block and sashing rows together to make the quilt top center.

Assembly Diagram

Inner Border

1. For the **inner border**, sew the dark red 3¹/₂" wide **strips** together end-to-end to make one continuous **inner border strip**. Cut 4 inner borders 56¹/₂" long from the inner border strip. Matching centers and corner, sew the side inner borders to the quilt top center. Press the seam allowances toward the borders.

2. Sew a navy **square F** to the ends of the remaining 2 borders. Press the seam allowances toward the border. Sew borders to the top and bottom of the quilt top center. Press the seam allowances toward the borders.

Appliqué Border

*Follow **Needle-Turn Appliqué**, page 36, or **Machine Appliqué**, page 37, to add the leaves and flowers.*

1. Use red **bias binding square**, follow **Making a Continuous Bias Strip**, page 43, to make a 1¹/₂" wide bias strip.

2. Matching wrong sides, fold strip in half and stitch ¹/₂" from fold forming a tube; trim seam allowance to ¹/₈". Press tube flat, centering seam allowance on back so raw edge isn't visible from front. Using ¹/₂" bias bar makes pressing faster and easier. Cut tube in half to make two vines.

3. Repeat Steps 1-2 using blue bias binding square.

4. Cut a strip of freezer paper 10" x 82". Create center registration lines by folding borders in half lengthwise and horizontally; crease firmly.

5. Referring to **Vine Placement Diagram,** mark 8" from either side of the center and crease. Repeat twice in each direction. On the outside edge of the center line, measure in 3" and mark (red mark on Diagram). At the first 8" increment from the center, measure in 3" from the inside edge and mark. Repeat this process 2 more times, referring to Diagram E. Repeat for the remaining end of the guide. On the dull side of the freezer paper, use a black pen or marker to draw a gentle curve to connect the marks.

Vine Placement Diagram

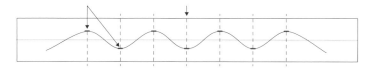

6. Center a cream **border strip** on top of the placement guide; pin. You should be able to see the placement guide through the fabric. Position the vine and baste in place with pins or small drops of fabric glue. ***Note:** If you press the vine with a little steam as you are positioning it will bend smoothly and lie flat.* Leaving about 12"-14" of vine unsewn at each end (vine ends will be attached after borders are sewn to quilt top), stitch vine in place by hand or machine. Pin loose vine ends out of the way of all seam allowances.

7. Referring to the **Border Diagram**, position flowers, flower centers, and leaves on a border. Do not place the last 2-3 leaves on each end of the border. These will be added after the borders are attached to the quilt top. Stitch in place by hand or machine. Make a total of 4 borders.

Border Diagram

8. Mark the center of each long edge of the quilt top and the center of each border. Match center marks and sew the borders to the quilt, stopping stitching $1/4$" from the ends. Miter the corners (**Figs. 7-8**).

Fig. 7

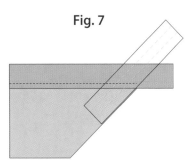

Fig. 8

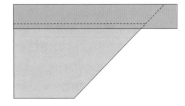

9. Position vine ends, overlapping them in the corners. Turning under the raw ends, stitch vines in place. Appliqué the remaining leaves in place.

Outer Border

1. For the **outer border**, sew the navy $3^{1}/_2$" wide **strips** together end-to-end to make one continuous **inner border strip**. Cut 4 outer borders $82^{1}/_2$" long from the outer border strip. Matching centers and corner, sew the side outer borders to the quilt top center. Press the seam allowances toward the borders.

2. Sew a pink and red **square F** to the ends of the remaining 2 borders. Press the seam allowances toward the border. Sew borders to the top and bottom of the quilt top center. Press the seam allowances toward the borders.

COMPLETING THE QUILT

1. Follow **Quilting**, page 38, to mark, layer, and quilt as desired. Quilt shown has feather quilting in the narrow borders and meander quilting in the appliqué border. The blocks are outline quilted around the stars and have meander quilting in the light background areas. The appliqués are outline quilted.

2. Follow **Making a Hanging Sleeve**, page 41, if a hanging sleeve is desired.

3. Use **binding strips** and follow **Binding**, page 41, to bind quilt.

It's Twirl Time

Finished Quilt Size: 44" x 54" (112 cm x 137 cm)
Finished Block Size: 10" x 10" (25 cm x 25 cm)

SHOPPING LIST

*Yardage is based on 43"/44" (109 cm/112 cm)
wide fabric with a usable width of 40" (102 cm).
Fat quarters are approximately 22" x 18" (56 cm x 46 cm).*

- ☐ 1¼ yds (1.1 m) total **or** 5-6 fat quarters of assorted light print fabrics for block backgrounds and inner border
- ☐ 1½ yds (1.4 m) total **or** 6 fat quarters of assorted dark print fabrics for blocks and outer borders
- ☐ ³⁄₈ yd (34 cm) of medium print fabric for block centers
- ☐ 2¼ yds (2.1 m) of fabric for backing
- ☐ ½ yd (57 cm) of fabric for binding
- ☐ 52" x 62" (132 cm x 157 cm) piece of batting

CUTTING THE PIECES

*Follow **Rotary Cutting**, page 34, to cut fabric. Cut all strips from the selvage-to-selvage width of the fabric. Cut strips from fat quarters parallel to the long edge. All measurements include $1/4$" seam allowances.*

From assorted light print fabrics:
- Cut a **total** of 170 **squares B** $2^1/_2$" x $2^1/_2$".
- Cut a **total** of 48 **rectangles C** $2^1/_2$" x $4^1/_2$".

From assorted dark print fabrics:
- Cut a **total** of 48 **squares A** $4^1/_2$" x $4^1/_2$".
- Cut 2 **border rectangles** $5^1/_2$" x $14^1/_2$".
- Cut 4 **border rectangles** $5^1/_2$" x $12^1/_2$".
- Cut 6 **border rectangles** $5^1/_2$" x $9^1/_2$".
- Cut 7 **border rectangles** $5^1/_2$" x $7^1/_2$".
- Cut 3 **border squares** $5^1/_2$" x $5^1/_2$".

From medium print fabric:
- Cut 60 **squares B** $2^1/_2$" x $2^1/_2$".

From binding fabric:
- Cut 6 **binding strips** $2^1/_4$" wide.

MAKING THE BLOCKS

*Follow **Piecing** and **Pressing**, page 35, to make the quilt top. Use $1/4$" seam allowances throughout.*

1. To make 2 Blocks, you will need:
   - 16 light print squares B
   - 8 light print rectangles C
   - 8 dark print squares A
   - 10 medium print squares B

2. Draw a diagonal line on the wrong side of 16 matching light print **squares B**. Place a square B on the corner of a dark print **square A**. Stitch on the drawn line (**Fig. 1**). trim seam allowance to $1/4$" (**Fig. 2**) and press open (**Fig. 3**).

Fig. 1

Fig. 2

Fig. 3

3. In the same manner, sew a light print square B to the opposite corner of the dark print square A (**Fig. 4**).

Fig. 4

4. Sew a medium print square B to a remaining corner of dark print square A to make **Unit 1**. Make 8 Unit 1's.

Unit 1 (make 8)

5. Sew a matching light print **rectangle C** to the left side of each Unit 1 to make **Unit 2**. Make 8 Unit 2's.

Unit 2 (make 8)

6. Arrange 4 Unit 2's and 1 medium square B as shown in **Block Diagram**. The Unit 1 positioned above the square B will be sewn to the square B with a partial seam (**Fig. 5**), indicated by the red dot. Once you have sewn the partial seam, continue adding Unit 1's clockwise (**Fig. 6**). Complete the partial seam to finish the block. Make 2 matching blocks.

Fig. 5

Fig. 6

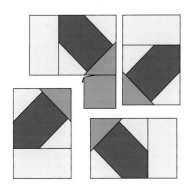

Block Diagram
(make 2)

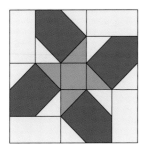

7. Repeat Steps 2-6 to make a total of 6 pairs of blocks (12 blocks total).

ASSEMBLING THE QUILT TOP
*Refer to **Quilt Top Diagram** to assemble the quilt top.*

1. To make quilt top center, arrange the Blocks in 4 rows of 3 blocks each. Sew the rows together.

2. To make 1 **inner side border**, sew together 20 light **squares B**, pressing seam allowances in 1 direction. Repeat to make a total of 2 inner side borders.

3. Sew 1 inner side border to each side of quilt top center.

4. To make 1 **inner top/bottom border**, sew together 17 light squares B, pressing seam allowances in 1 direction. Repeat to make a total of 2 inner top/ bottom borders.

5. Sew inner top/bottom borders to quilt top center.

6. For the outer borders, sew assorted dark print **border rectangles** and **squares** together end to end. From this piece, cut 4 **outer borders** 44$^{1}/_{2}$" long.

7. Sew 1 outer border to each side of the quilt top; press seam allowances toward the borders. Sew top and bottom outer border to the quilt top; press seam allowances toward the borders.

Quilt Top Diagram

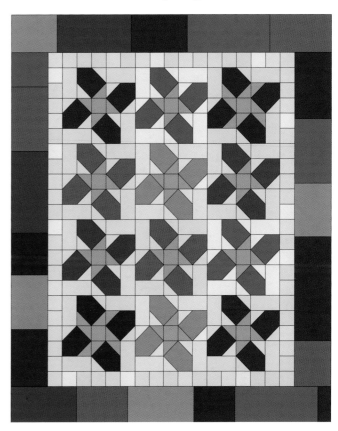

COMPLETING THE QUILT

1. Follow **Quilting**, page 38, to mark, layer, and quilt as desired. Quilt shown is quilted with a large leaf and vine pattern in the outer border and a zigzag in the inner border. The blocks have swirls in the center star, large leaves in the petals, and a small leaf and vine in the background.

2. Follow **Making a Hanging Sleeve**, page 41, if a hanging sleeve is desired.

3. Use **binding strips** and follow **Binding**, page 41, to bind quilt.

Pinwheel Tapestry

Finished Quilt Size: 87" x 96" (221 cm x 244 cm)
Finished Block Size: 9" x 9" (23 cm x 23 cm)

SHOPPING LIST

Yardage is based on 43"/44" (109 cm/112 cm) wide fabric with a usable width of 40" (102 cm). Fat quarters are approximately 22" x 18" (56 cm x 46 cm).

- ☐ 27 fat quarters of assorted tan, brown, red, and black prints for blocks and Flying Geese border
- ☐ 14 fat quarters of assorted light prints for block backgrounds and Flying Geese border
- ☐ 1 yd (91 cm) of black solid fabric for narrow borders
- ☐ 2½ yds (2.3 m) of red paisley print fabric for outer border and blocks
- ☐ 8 yds (7.3 m) of fabric for backing
- ☐ 1 yd (91 cm) of brown print fabric for binding
- ☐ 95" x 104" (241 cm x 264 cm) piece of batting

CUTTING THE PIECES

Note: To achieve the scrappy look of our quilt, you may want to mix and match the print fabrics and background fabrics. We also used some of the red paisley border fabric in our blocks. Cut your borders and binding first to ensure that you have enough fabric.

Follow Rotary Cutting, page 34, to cut fabric. Cut all strips from the selvage-to-selvage width of the fabric. Cut strips from fat quarters parallel to the long edge. Borders are cut exact length. All measurements include 1/4" seam allowances.

From assorted dark print fat quarters:
- Cut 56 matching sets of 4 **rectangles A** 7" x 3".
- Cut 56 **squares C** 4 1/2" x 4 1/2".

From assorted light print fat quarters:
- Cut 56 matching sets of 8 **squares B** 3" x 3".

From black solid fabric:
- Cut 16 **strips** 2" wide.

From red paisley print fabric:
- Cut 2 *lengthwise* **side outer borders** 6" x 84 1/2".
- Cut 2 *lengthwise* **top/bottom outer borders** 6" x 87 1/2".

From brown print fabric for binding:
- Cut 10 **binding strips** 2 1/2" wide.

MAKING THE BLOCKS

Follow Piecing and Pressing, page 35, to make the quilt top. Use 1/4" seam allowances throughout. As you stitch the units for the Pinwheel Blocks, you will also be sewing "bonus" Triangle-Squares which will be used to make the pieced border. Set these aside to use in border construction.

1. For each block, you will need:
   - 4 matching medium/dark print **rectangles A**.
   - 8 matching light print **squares B**.
   - 1 medium/dark print **square C**

2. Draw a diagonal line on the wrong side of each square B.

3. Matching right sides, place 1 square B on the left edge of 1 rectangle A. Stitch on the drawn line. Then stitch a scant 1/2" from the drawn line (**Fig. 1**).

Fig. 1

4. Cut between the stitched lines (**Fig. 2**) to make 1 **Triangle-Square** and 1 **Unit 1**. Press the seam allowances toward the darker fabric. Make 4 Unit 1's and 4 Triangle-Squares. Set aside the Triangle-Squares for the Flying Geese Border.

Fig. 2

Triangle-Square (make 4)   **Unit1** (make 4)

5. In the same manner, stitch a light print square B to the right edge of Unit 1 **(Fig. 3)** to make **Unit 2** and a Triangle-Square. Make 4 Unit 2's and 4 Triangle-Squares. Set aside the Triangle-Squares for the Flying Geese Border.

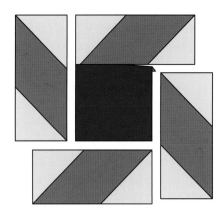

Fig. 3

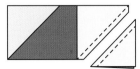

Unit 2 (make 4)

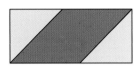

6. Referring to the **Assembly Diagram**, arrange 4 matching Unit 2's and 1 contrasting **square C**. The first seam will be a partial seam because you will only sew it part of the way. Sew a square C to a Unit 2 , stopping about 1 1/2"-2" from the end of the seam **(Fig. 4)**. Finger-press the seam allowances toward the square C. Working counter clockwise, sew the remaining 3 Unit 2's to square C. When you have sewn on the last unit, finish the partial seam to complete the **Pinwheel Block**.

Pinwheel Block

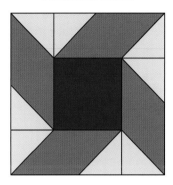

Fig. 4

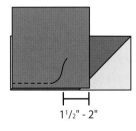

1 1/2" - 2"

7. Repeat Steps 1-6 to make a total of 56 Blocks.

ASSEMBLING THE QUILT TOP

*Refer to **Quilt Top Diagram** to assemble the quilt top.*

1. Arrange and then sew the Blocks into 8 rows of 7 blocks each to make the quilt top center.

2. For the **inner narrow border**, sew the solid black **strips** together end-to-end to make one continuous **narrow border strip**. Cut 2 side inner narrow borders 72½" long and 2 top/bottom inner narrow borders 66½" long from the narrow border strip. Matching centers and corner, sew the side then top/bottom inner narrow borders to the quilt top center.

3. For the **Flying Geese Border**, trim 392 Triangle-Squares to 2" x 2". Sew 2 Triangle-Squares together to make a **Flying Geese Unit**. Make a total of 196 Flying Geese Units.

Flying Geese Unit
(make 196)

4. Sew 50 Flying Geese Units together to make a **Flying Geese Side Border**. Make 2 Flying Geese Side Borders. Referring to the photo for the correct orientation, sew 1 Flying Geese Side Border to each side of the quilt. Press the seam allowances toward the first inner borders.

5. Sew 44 Flying Geese together to make the **Flying Geese Top Border**. Repeat for the **Flying Geese Bottom Border**.

6. Sew together 2 Flying Geese Units to make a **Double Geese Block**. Make a total of 4 Double Geese Blocks.

Double Geese Block
(make 4)

7. Sew a Double Geese Block to each end of the Flying Geese top and bottom borders. Referring to the photo for the correct orientation of the borders, stitch the borders to the quilt. Press the seam allowances toward the solid black borders.

8. Cut 2 **side outer narrow borders** 81½" long and 2 **top/bottom outer narrow borders** 75½" long from the narrow border strip. Matching centers and corner, sew the side then top/bottom outer narrow borders to the quilt top center.

9. Matching centers and corner, sew the side then top/bottom outer borders to the quilt top center.

COMPLETING THE QUILT

1. Follow **Quilting**, page 38, to mark, layer, and quilt as desired. Quilt shown has meandering quilting in the light color block backgrounds. The dark pinwheels and the Flying Geese Border are outline quilted with curved lines. The narrow borders have a wavy feather design and the outer border has channel quilting spaced about 1½" apart.

2. Follow **Making a Hanging Sleeve**, page 41, if a hanging sleeve is desired.

3. Use **binding strips** and follow **Binding**, page 41, to bind quilt.

Quilt Top Diagram

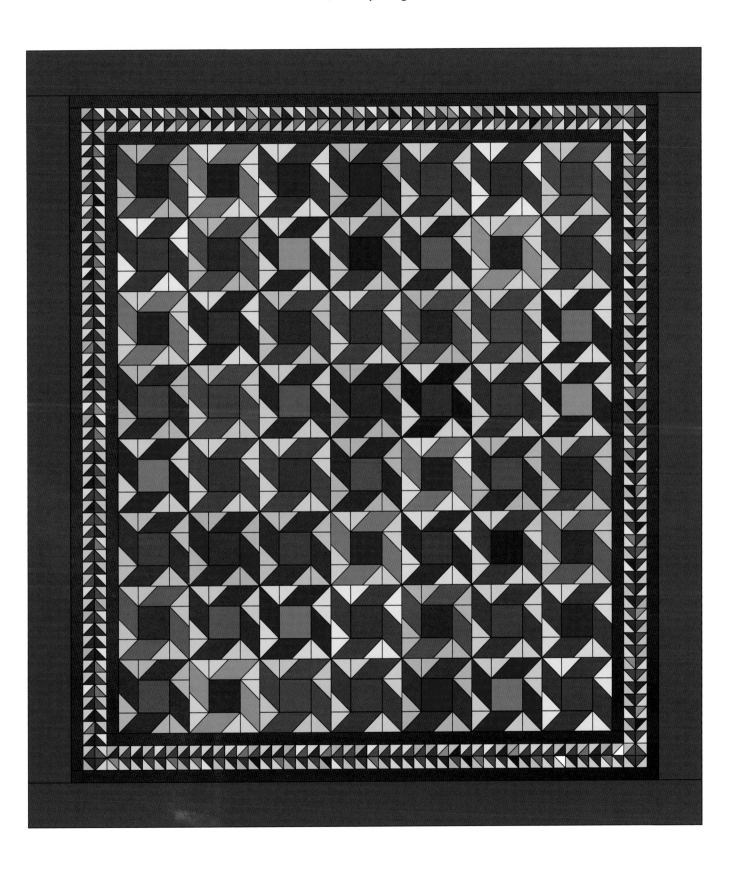

Stars of The Old West

Finished Quilt Size: 85¹/₂" x 97¹/₂" (217 cm x 248 cm)
Finished Block Size: 12" x 12" (30 cm x 30 cm)

SHOPPING LIST

*Yardage is based on 43"/44" (109 cm/112 cm)
wide fabric with a usable width of 40" (102 cm).*

- ☐ 3³/₄ - 4¹/₄ yds (3.4 m - 3.9 m) **total** of assorted cream/tan print fabrics for block backgrounds
- ☐ 3¹/₈ - 3⁵/₈ yds (2.9 m - 3.1 m) **total** of assorted medium/dark print fabrics for appliqués
- ☐ 3 - 3¹/₂ yds (2.7 m - 3.2 m) **total** of assorted light/medium print fabrics for appliqués
- ☐ 2⁷/₈ yds (2.6 m) of cream small print fabric for inner border
- ☐ 2⁷/₈ yds (26 m) of tan small print fabric for inner border
- ☐ 1 yd (91 cm) of rust small print fabric for vine appliqué
- ☐ 1¹/₄ yds (1.1 m) of black/red print fabric for outer border
- ☐ 7⁷/₈ yds (7.2 m) of fabric for backing
- ☐ 1 yd (91 cm) of black print fabric for binding
- ☐ freezer paper - 1 strip 9¹/₂" x 96" and 1 strip 9¹/₂" x 84"
- ☐ template plastic for Needle-Turn Appliqué´**or** paper-backed fusible web for Machine Appliqué
- ☐ ¹/₂" wide (12 mm) bias press bar
- ☐ 94" x 106" (239 cm x 269 cm) piece of batting

CUTTING THE PIECES

*Follow **Rotary Cutting**, page 34, to cut fabric. Cut all strips from the selvage-to-selvage width of the fabric. Borders are cut longer than needed and will be trimmed to fit quilt top center. All measurements include 1/4" seam allowances.*

From assorted cream/tan print fabrics:
- Cut a total of 120 **squares** 6¹/₂" x 6¹/₂".

From *each* of cream small print fabric and tan small print fabric:
- Cut 2 *lengthwise* **appliqué border strips** 9¹/₂" x 96".
- Cut 2 *lengthwise* **appliqué border strips** 9¹/₂" x 84".

From rust small print fabric:
- Cut 1 **square** 32" x 32".

From black/red print fabric:
- Cut 10 strips 3³/₄" wide. Piece these strips together end to end. From this strip, cut 4 **outer borders** 3³/₄" x 98".

From black print fabric for binding:
- Cut 10 **binding strips** 2¹/₂" wide.

CUTTING THE APPLIQUÉS

*You can hand or machine appliqué the circles, stars, vine, and leaves. Use patterns, page 45-46, and follow **Making and Using Templates**, page 36, for hand appliqué **or** follow **Preparing Fusible Appliqués**, page 37, for machine appliqué.*

From assorted medium/dark print fabrics:
- Cut 18 **circle A's**.
- Cut 12 **star B's**.
- Cut 31 **leaf C's**; cut 32 **leaf C's** in reverse.
- Cut 4 **leaf D's**; cut 1 **leaf D** in reverse.

From assorted light/medium print fabrics:
- Cut 12 **circle A's**.
- Cut 18 **star B's**.
- Cut 22 **leaf C's**; cut 24 **leaf C's** in reverse.
- Cut 3 **leaf D's** in reverse.

MAKING THE BLOCKS

*Follow **Piecing** and **Pressing**, page 35, to make the quilt top. Use 1/4" seam allowances throughout. Follow **Needle-Turn Appliqué**, page 36, or **Machine Appliqué**, page 37, to add the appliqué pieces.*

1. Sew 4 assorted cream/tan print squares together to make **Unit 1**. Make 30 Unit 1's.

Unit 1
(make 30)

2. Using seams as placement guides, center 1 medium/dark print **circle A** and 1 light/medium **star B** on Unit 1. Appliqué in place to make **Star Block A**. Make a total of 18 Star Block A's.

Star Block A
(make 18)

3. In the same manner, center 1 light/medium **circle A** and 1 medium/dark **star B** on Unit 1. Appliqué in place to make **Star Block B**. Make a total of 12 Star Block B's.

Star Block B
(make 12)

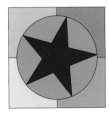

ASSEMBLING THE QUILT TOP

1. Sew blocks together in 6 rows of 5 blocks each. Sew rows together to make the quilt top center.

2. Measure length and width of your quilt top center from raw edge to raw edge, through the centers. Subtract 1/2" from each measurement. Record these finished measurements.

3. To make the **border stitching guide**, place the dull side of the 84" long freezer paper strip right side up and finger-press in half both length and width; open strip and mark fold lines with pencil. Measure the finished width of your quilt onto the paper, centering on vertical penciled line, and mark ends with vertical lines (as indicated by red lines on diagram).

4. Fold center section of strip (between red lines) into **thirds** and mark (blue lines on diagram). Fold each of 3 center sections in half and mark (green lines on diagram). Label inside and outside edges as shown.

Unit 2

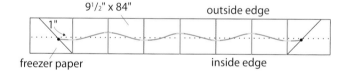

5. Referring to **Fig. 1**, align 45°-angle line on ruler with inside edge of paper. Starting at bottom of red line, draw diagonal line. Repeat at opposite end of strip, as shown in Unit 2.

Fig. 1

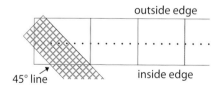

6. Beginning at lower end of diagonal line, measure 5 1/2" along line and mark (**Fig. 2**). Repeat on other end of strip.

Fig. 2

7. Beginning at left (red) line on 84" strip, make a short mark (brown on Unit 2) 1" below center horizontal line (dotted on Unit 2). Mark 1" above center line at next vertical line (green). Continue in this manner to make marks below and above center line as shown. Beginning at mark on diagonal line, draw a smooth curved line, connecting the short marks and ending at mark on remaining diagonal line. Mark straight lines connecting curved line with ends of strip.

8. In the same manner and referring to **Unit 3**, fold and mark 96" freezer paper strip using measurement of the finished length of your quilt (red lines on Unit 3). Fold center section of strip into **fourths** and mark (blue lines on diagram). Fold each center section in half and mark (green lines in diagram). Draw diagonal lines and mark at 5 1/2". Mark curving line on 96" strip with straight lines at each end.

Unit 3

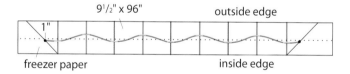

9. Cut 84" paper strip along curved line. Discard the portion nearest to the **inside** edge. The remaining portion is the stitching guide for top and bottom borders. In the same manner, cut 96" strip along curved line and discard the portion nearest the **inside** edge. The remaining portion is the stitching guide for side borders.

Piecing the Inner Border

1. Referring to **Fig. 3**, press 84" stitching guide to **right side** of cream small print 84" strip, aligning edges.

Fig. 3

2. Place prepared cream strip on top of tan small print 84" strip, **both strips right side up**. Pin strips together along edges. Stitch along curved edge of guide, being careful not to stitch through paper. Remove pins; carefully remove guide to use again. Cut away **outside** portion of cream fabric, leaving $1/4$" seam allowance (**Fig. 4**) and exposing tan fabric beneath (**Fig. 5**), to make **top/bottom inner border strip**. (If you wish, cut away underlying **inside** portion of tan fabric, leaving $1/4$" seam allowance.) Exposed seam allowance will be covered by vine when appliqués are add. Repeat to make second top/bottom inner border strip.

Fig. 4

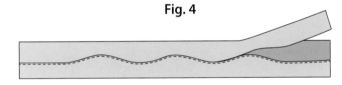

Fig. 5

3. Repeat Steps 1-2 to make a 96" long **side inner border strip**. Make 2 side inner border strips.

Assembling and Appliquéing the Quilt Top

1. Center and pin inner border strips to sides, top, and bottom of quilt. Starting and stopping $1/4$" from quilt corners and backstitching to secure, sew strips to quilt center. Press seam allowances toward quilt center. Fold quilt on diagonal, right sides together (**Fig. 6**). Align border strip raw edges and border seams at the $1/4$" backstitched point; pin together. Align ruler edge with fold, extending ruler completely across border. Draw line from the backstitched point to the border raw edges. Stitch on drawn line, backstitching at both ends. Press seam open. With quilt right side up, align 45°-angle line of square ruler on seamline to check accuracy. If corner is flat and square, trim excess fabric to $1/4$" seam allowance. Repeat for all corners.

Fig. 6

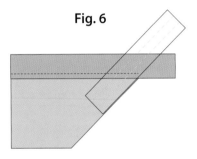

2. Use rust small print **square** and follow **Making a Continuous Bias Strip**, page 43, to make a $1^{1}/_{2}$" x 340" bias strip.

3. Fold strip in half, wrong sides together (**Fig. 7**). Stitch $1/2$" from fold. Trim seam allowance to $1/8$". Press tube flat, centering seam allowance on back so raw edge isn't visible from front. Using $1/2$" bias press bar makes pressing faster and easier. Cut 2 strips 90" long and 2 strips 80" long.

Fig. 7

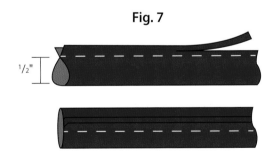

Quilt Top Diagram

4. Referring to **Quilt Top Diagram** and keeping in mind outer $1/4$" seam allowances, position rust bias vines over the curved seams. Appliqué in place, trimming and turning under ends as needed. Position the leaves along the vine and appliqué in place.

5. Stitch 1 outer border to each side edge; trim even with top/bottom. Sew the remaining outer borders to the top/bottom edges; trim even with sides.

COMPLETING THE QUILT

1. Follow **Quilting**, page 38, to mark, layer, and quilt as desired. Quilt shown is quilted with a star motif in each star and curlicues between star points. Block backgrounds are filled with feathers. The vines and leaves are outline quilted and the border background has meandering. The outer border is stitched with parallel lines at right angles to the quilt edge.

2. Follow **Making a Hanging Sleeve**, page 41, if a hanging sleeve is desired.

3. Use **binding strips** and follow **Binding**, page 41, to bind quilt.

Welcome Inn

Finished Quilt Size: 33" x 33" (84 cm x 84 cm)
Finished Appliqué Block Size: 15" x 15" (38 cm x 38 cm)

SHOPPING LIST

Yardage is based on 43"/44" (109 cm/112 cm) wide fabric with a usable width of 40" (102 cm). Fat quarters are approximately 22" x 18" (56 cm x 46 cm).

- ☐ 1 fat quarter of natural muslin fabric for background
- ☐ 1 fat quarter of rust print fabric for inner border
- ☐ ½ yd (46 cm) of green print fabric for appliqués and large triangles
- ☐ ⅝ yd (57 cm) of gold print fabric for appliqués, inner border, and binding
- ☐ ⅞ yd (80 cm) of black/tan print fabric for appliqués and outer border
- ☐ 1⅛ yds (1 m) of backing fabric
- ☐ template plastic for Needle-Turn Appliqué **or**
  paper-backed fusible web for Machine Appliqué
- ☐ 37" x 37" (94 cm x 94 cm) piece of batting

CUTTING THE PIECES

*Follow **Rotary Cutting**, page 34, to cut fabric. Cut all strips from the selvage-to-selvage width of the fabric. Cut strips from fat quarters parallel to the long edge. Borders are cut exact length. All measurements include ¹/₄" seam allowances.*

From natural muslin fabric fat quarter:
- Cut 1 **background** 16¹/₂" x 16¹/₂".

From rust print fat quarter:
- Cut 2 strips 3¹/₄" wide. From these strips, cut 8 **rectangles H** 3¹/₄" x 6".

From green print fabric:
- Cut 1 strip 12³/₄" wide. From this strip, cut 2 squares 12³/₄" x 12³/₄". Cut each square *once* diagonally to make 4 **triangles G**.

From gold print fabric:
- Cut 1 strip 3¹/₄" wide. From this strip, cut 4 **squares J** 3¹/₄" x 3¹/₄".
- Cut 2 strips 3¹/₄" wide. From these strips, cut 8 **rectangles H** 3¹/₄" x 6".
- Cut 4 **binding strips** 2¹/₄" wide.

From black/tan print fabric:
- Cut 3 strips 3¹/₄" wide. From these strips, cut 32 **squares J** 3¹/₄" x 3¹/₄".
- Cut 2 **side borders** 3¹/₂" x 28".
- Cut 2 **top/bottom borders** 3¹/₂" x 34".

CUTTING THE APPLIQUÉS

*You can hand or machine appliqué your quilt. Use the patterns, page 44, and follow **Making and Using Templates**, page 36, for hand appliqué **or** follow **Preparing Fusible Appliqués**, page 37, for machine appliqué .*

From rust print fat quarter:
- Cut 4 **F's**.

From green print fabric:
- Cut 4 **A's**.
- Cut 4 **B's** and 4 **B's in reverse**.

From gold print fabric:
- Cut 4 **E's**.

From black/tan print fabric:
- Cut 1 **D**.
- Cut 4 **C's**.

MAKING THE BLOCKS

*Follow **Piecing** and **Pressing**, page 35, to make the quilt top. Use ¹/₄" seam allowances throughout. Follow **Needle-Turn Appliqué**, page 36, or **Machine Appliqué**, page 37, to add the appliqué pieces.*

Appliqué Block
1. Working from the background up, sew appliqué pieces **A** through **F** to the **background**.

2. Press the background from the wrong side and trim to 15¹/₂" x 15¹/₂" to complete the **Appliqué Block**.

Appliqué Block

3. Sew 1 **triangle G** to each side of the **Appliqué Block** to complete the quilt top center.

Flying Geese Blocks

1. Draw a diagonal line on the wrong side of each **square J**. Matching right sides, place a square J on one end of a rust or gold **rectangle H** and stitch on the drawn line. Trim ¹/₄" from stitching line (**Fig. 1**); press open (**Fig. 2**).

Fig. 1

Fig. 2

2. Repeat on the opposite end of rectangle H (**Fig. 3**) to make a **Flying Geese Block**. Make 8 rust and 8 gold Flying Geese Blocks.

Fig. 3

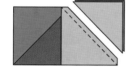

Flying Geese Block (make 8 rust and 8 gold)

ASSEMBLING THE QUILT TOP

*Refer to the **Quilt Top Diagram** to assemble quilt top.*

1. Sew together 2 rust Flying Geese Blocks and 2 gold Flying Geese Blocks to make a **Flying Geese Border**. Make 4 Flying Geese Borders.

Flying Geese Border
(make 4)

2. Sew 1 Flying Geese Border to each side of the quilt top center. Press seam allowances toward the border.

3. Sew 1 **square J** to each end of the remaining Flying Geese Borders. Press seam allowances toward borders. Sew 1 border to the top and 1 border to the bottom of the quilt top center.

4. Sew 1 **side border** to each side of the quilt top. Sew the **top/bottom borders** to the quilt top. Press seam allowances toward the borders.

Quilt Top Diagram

COMPLETING THE QUILT

1. Follow **Quilting**, page 38, to mark, layer, and quilt as desired. Quilt shown is outline quilted around the appliqués and the block background is quilted with tight swirl. The green triangles are quilted with a feather in each triangle.

2. Follow **Making a Hanging Sleeve**, page 41, if a hanging sleeve is desired.

3. Use **binding strips** and follow **Binding**, page 41, to bind quilt.

GENERAL INSTRUCTIONS

To make your quilting easier and more enjoyable, we encourage you to carefully read all of the general instructions, study the color photographs, and familiarize yourself with the individual project instructions before beginning a project.

FABRICS

Selecting Fabrics

Choose high-quality, medium-weight 100% cotton fabrics. All-cotton fabrics hold a crease better, fray less, and are easier to quilt than cotton/polyester blends.

Yardage requirements listed for each project are based on 43"/44" wide fabric with a "usable" width of 40" after shrinkage and trimming selvages. Actual usable width will probably vary slightly from fabric to fabric. Our recommended yardage lengths should be adequate for occasional re-squaring of fabric when many cuts are required.

Preparing Fabrics

Pre-washing fabrics may cause edges to ravel. As a result, your fat quarters may not be large enough to cut all of the pieces required for your chosen project. Therefore, we do not recommend pre-washing yardage or fat quarters.

Before cutting, prepare fabrics with a steam iron set on cotton and starch or sizing. The starch or sizing will give the fabric a crisp finish. This will make cutting more accurate and may make piecing easier.

ROTARY CUTTING
Cutting From Yardage

- Place fabric on work surface with fold closest to you.

- Cut all strips from the selvage-to-selvage width of the fabric unless otherwise indicated in project instructions.

- Square left edge of fabric using rotary cutter and rulers (**Figs. 1-2**).

Fig. 1

Fig. 2

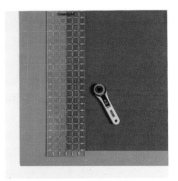

- To cut each strip required for a project, place ruler over cut edge of fabric, aligning desired marking on ruler with cut edge; make cut (**Fig. 3**).

Fig. 3

- When cutting several strips from a single piece of fabric, it is important to make sure that cuts remain at a perfect right angle to the fold; square fabric as needed.

Cutting From Fat Quarters

- If cutting strips parallel to the long edge, place fat quarter on work surface with short edge closest to you. Cut all strips parallel to the long edge of the fabric in the same manner as cutting from yardage unless otherwise indicated in project instructions.

- To cut each strip, place ruler over cut edge of fabric, aligning desired marking on ruler with cut edge; make the cut.

PIECING

Precise cutting, followed by accurate piecing, will ensure that all pieces of quilt top fit together well.

- Set sewing machine stitch length for approximately 11 stitches per inch.

- Use neutral-colored general-purpose sewing thread (not quilting thread) in needle and in bobbin.

- An accurate 1/4" seam allowance is essential. Presser feet that are 1/4" wide are available for most sewing machines.

- When piecing, always place pieces right sides together and match raw edges; pin if necessary.

- Chain piecing saves time and will usually result in more accurate piecing.

- Trim away points of seam allowances that extend beyond edges of sewn pieces.

Sewing Strip Sets

When there are several strips to assemble into a strip set, first sew strips together into pairs, then sew pairs together to form strip set. To help avoid distortion, sew seams in opposite directions (**Fig. 4**).

Fig. 4

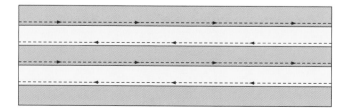

Sewing Across Seam Intersections

When sewing across intersection of two seams, place pieces right sides together and match seams exactly, making sure seam allowances are pressed in opposite directions (**Fig. 5**).

Fig. 5

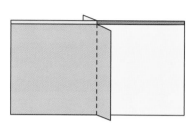

Sewing Sharp Points

To ensure sharp points when joining triangular or diagonal pieces, stitch across the center of the "X" (shown in pink) formed on wrong side by previous seams (**Fig. 6**).

Fig. 6

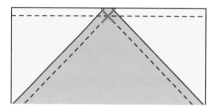

PRESSING

- Use steam iron set on "Cotton" for all pressing.

- Press after sewing each seam.

- Seam allowances are almost always pressed to one side, usually toward darker fabric. However, to reduce bulk it may be necessary to press seam allowances toward the lighter fabric or even to press them open.

- To prevent dark fabric seam allowance from showing through light fabric, trim darker seam allowance slightly narrower than lighter seam allowance.

- To press long seams without curving or other distortion, lay strips across width of the ironing board.

- When sewing blocks into rows, seam allowances may be pressed in one direction in odd numbered rows and in the opposite direction in even numbered rows. When sewing rows together, press seam allowances in one direction.

MAKING AND USING TEMPLATES

1. To make a template from a pattern, use a permanent fine-point pen to carefully trace the pattern onto template plastic, making sure to transfer all markings Cut out the template along the outer drawn line. Check the template against the original pattern for accuracy.

2. Place template on the right side of appliqué fabric. Lightly draw around template with pencil, leaving at least 1/2" between shapes. Repeat for number of shapes specified in project instructions.

3. Cut out shapes approximately 3/16" outside drawn line. Clip inside curves and points to, but not through, drawn line.

NEEDLE-TURN APPLIQUÉ

Using needle to turn under seam allowance while blindstitching appliqué to background fabric is called "needle-turn appliqué."

1. Arrange shapes on background fabric and pin or baste in place.

2. Thread a sharps needle with a single strand of general-purpose sewing thread that matches appliqué; knot one end.

3. Begin blindstitching on as straight an edge as possible, turning a small section of seam allowance to wrong side with needle, concealing drawn line (**Fig. 7**).

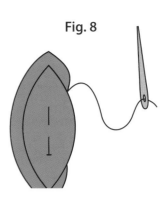

Fig. 8

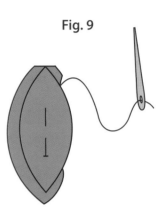

Fig. 9

5. To stitch inward point, stitch to 1/2" from point (**Fig. 10**). Clip to but not through seam allowance at point (**Fig. 11**). Turn seam allowance under between stitching and point. Stitch to point, taking two or three stitches at point to secure. Turn under small amount of seam allowance past point and resume stitching.

Fig. 7

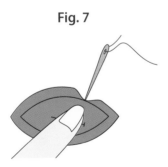

4. To stitch outward points, stitch to 1/2" from point (**Fig. 8**). Turn seam allowance under at point (**Fig. 9**); then turn remainder of seam allowance between stitching and point. Stitch to point, taking two or three stitches at top of point to secure. Turn under small amount of seam allowance past point and resume stitching.

Fig. 10

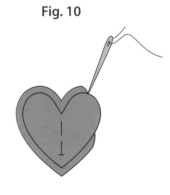

Fig. 11

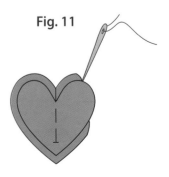

6. Do not turn under or stitch seam allowances that will be covered by other appliqué pieces.

7. To appliqué pressed bias strips, baste strips in place and blindstitch along edges.

8. To reduce bulk, background fabric behind appliqués may be cut away. After stitching appliqués in place, turn block over and use sharp scissors or specially designed appliqué scissors to trim away background fabric approximately $3/16$" from stitching line. Take care not to cut appliqué fabric or stitches.

PREPARING FUSIBLE APPLIQUÉS

White or light-colored fabrics may need to be lined with fusible interfacing before applying fusible web to prevent darker fabrics from showing through.

1. Place paper-backed fusible web, paper side up, over appliqué pattern. Trace pattern onto paper side of web with pencil as many times as indicated in project instructions for a single fabric.

2. Follow manufacturer's instructions to fuse traced patterns to wrong side of fabrics. Do not remove paper backing.

3. Use scissors to cut out appliqué pieces along traced lines. Remove paper backing from all pieces.

MACHINE APPLIQUÉ

The exposed raw edges of the fused appliqué pieces in this book are finished with zigzag stitching using a medium stitch length and a medium stitch width.

1. Pin stabilizer, such as paper or any of the commercially available products, on wrong side of background fabric before stitching appliqués in place.

2. Thread sewing machine with general-purpose thread; use general-purpose thread that matches background fabric in bobbin.

3. Set sewing machine for a medium (approximately $1/8$") zigzag stitch and a medium stitch length. Slightly loosening the top tension may yield a smoother stitch.

4. Begin by stitching two or three stitches in place (drop feed dogs or set stitch length at 0) to anchor thread. Most of the zigzag stitch should be on the appliqué with the right edge of the stitch falling at the outside edge of the appliqué. Stitch over all exposed raw edges of appliqué pieces.

5. (**Note**: Dots on **Figs. 12-17** indicate where to leave needle in fabric when pivoting.) For outside corners, stitch just past corner, stopping with needle in background fabric (**Fig. 12**). Raise presser foot. Pivot project, lower presser foot, and stitch adjacent side (**Fig. 13**).

Fig. 12

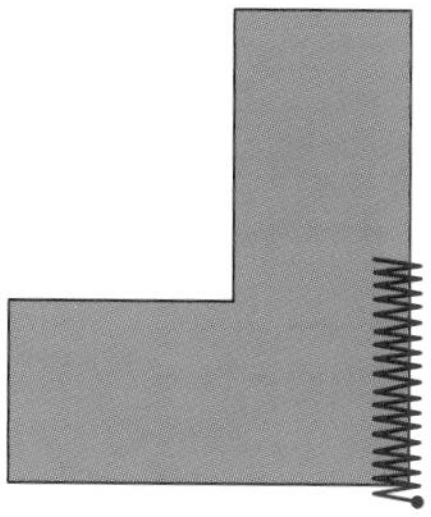

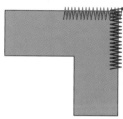

Fig. 13

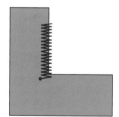

6. For inside corners, stitch just past corner, stopping with needle in appliqué fabric (**Fig. 14**). Raise presser foot. Pivot project, lower presser foot, and stitch adjacent side (**Fig. 15**).

Fig. 14

Fig. 15

7. When stitching outside curves, stop with needle in background fabric. Raise presser foot and pivot project as needed. Lower presser foot and continue stitching, pivoting as often as necessary to follow curve (**Fig. 16**).

Fig. 16

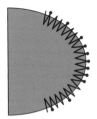

8. When stitching inside curves, stop with needle in appliqué fabric. Raise presser foot and pivot project as needed. Lower presser foot and continue stitching, pivoting as often as necessary to follow curve (**Fig. 17**).

Fig. 17

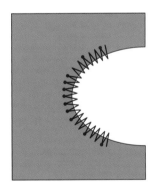

9. Do not backstitch at end of stitching. Pull threads to wrong side of background fabric; knot thread and trim ends.
10. Carefully tear away stabilizer.

QUILTING

Quilting holds the three layers (top, batting, and backing) of the quilt together and can be done by hand or machine. Because marking, layering, and quilting are interrelated and may be done in different orders depending on circumstances, please read entire Quilting section, pages 38-40, before beginning project.

Types of Quilting designs

In the Ditch Quilting

Quilting along seamlines or along edges of appliquéd pieces is called "in the ditch" quilting. This type of quilting should be done on side opposite seam allowance and does not have to be marked.

Outline Quilting

Quilting a consistent distance, usually $1/4$", from seam or appliqué is called "outline" quilting. Outline quilting may be marked, or $1/4$" masking tape may be placed along seamlines for quilting guide. (Do not leave tape on quilt longer than necessary, since it may leave an adhesive residue.)

Motif Quilting

Quilting a design, such as a feathered wreath, is called "motif" quilting. This type of quilting should be marked before basting quilt layers together.

Echo Quilting

Quilting that follows the outline of an appliquéd or pieced design with two or more parallel lines is called "echo" quilting. This type of quilting does not need to be marked.

Channel Quilting

Quilting with straight, parallel lines is called "channel" quilting. This type of quilting may be marked or stitched using a guide.

Crosshatch Quilting

Quilting straight lines in a grid pattern is called "crosshatch" quilting. Lines may be stitched parallel to edges of quilt or stitched diagonally. This type of quilting may be marked or stitched using a guide.

Meandering Quilting

Quilting in random curved lines and swirls is called "meandering" quilting. Quilting lines should not cross or touch each other. This type of quilting does not need to be marked.

Stipple Quilting

Meandering quilting that is very closely spaced is called "stipple" quilting. Stippling will flatten the area quilted and is often stitched in background areas to raise appliquéd or pieced designs. This type of quilting does not need to be marked.

Marking Quilting Lines

Quilting lines may be marked using fabric marking pencils, chalk markers, or water- or air-soluble pens.

Simple quilting designs may be marked with chalk or chalk pencil after basting. A small area may be marked, then quilted, before moving to next area to be marked. Intricate designs should be marked before basting using a more durable marker.

Caution: Pressing may permanently set some marks. Test different markers on scrap fabric to find one that marks clearly and can be thoroughly removed.

A wide variety of pre-cut quilting stencils, as well as entire books of quilting patterns, are available. Using a stencil makes it easier to mark intricate or repetitive designs.

To make a stencil from a pattern, center template plastic over pattern and use a permanent marker to trace pattern onto plastic. Use a craft knife with single or double blade to cut channels along traced lines (**Fig. 18**).

Fig. 18

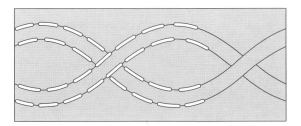

Preparing The Backing

To allow for slight shifting of quilt top during quilting, backing should be approximately 4" larger on all sides. Yardage requirements listed for quilt backings are calculated for 43"/44"w fabric. Using 90"w or 108"w fabric for the backing of a bed-sized quilt may eliminate piecing. To piece a backing using 43"/44"w fabric, use the following instructions.

1. Measure length and width of quilt top; add 8" to each measurement.
2. If determined width is 79" or less, cut backing fabric into two lengths slightly longer than determined length measurement. Trim selvages. Place lengths with right sides facing and sew long edges together, forming tube (**Fig. 19**). Match seams and press along one fold (**Fig. 20**). Cut along pressed fold to form single piece (**Fig. 21**).

| **Fig. 19** | **Fig. 20** | **Fig. 21** |

3. If determined width is more than 79", it may require less fabric yardage if the backing is pieced horizontally. Divide determined length measurement by 40" to determine how many widths will be needed. Cut required number of widths the determined width measurement. Trim selvages. Sew long edges together to form single piece.
4. Trim backing to size determined in Step 1; press seam allowances open.

Choosing The Batting

The appropriate batting will make quilting easier. For fine hand quilting, choose low-loft batting. All cotton or cotton/polyester blend battings work well for machine quilting because the cotton helps "grip" quilt layers. If quilt is to be tied, a high-loft batting, sometimes called extra-loft or fat batting, may be used to make quilt "fluffy."

Types of batting include cotton, polyester, wool, cotton/polyester blend, cotton/wool blend, and silk.

When selecting batting, refer to package labels for characteristics and care instructions. Cut batting same size as prepared backing.

Assembling The Quilt

1. Examine wrong side of quilt top closely; trim any seam allowances and clip any threads that may show through front of the quilt. Press quilt top, being careful not to "set" any marked quilting lines.
2. Place backing wrong side up on flat surface. Use masking tape to tape edges of backing to surface. Place batting on top of backing fabric. Smooth batting gently, being careful not to stretch or tear. Center quilt top right side up on batting.
3. Use 1" rustproof safety pins to "pin-baste" all layers together, spacing pins approximately 4" apart. Begin at center and work toward outer edges to secure all layers. If possible, place pins away from areas that will be quilted, although pins may be removed as needed when quilting.

Machine Quilting Methods

Use general-purpose thread in bobbin. Do not use quilting thread. Thread the needle of machine with general-purpose thread or transparent monofilament thread to make quilting blend with quilt top fabrics. Use decorative thread, such as a metallic or contrasting-color general-purpose thread, to make quilting lines stand out more.

Straight-Line Quilting

The term "straight-line" is somewhat deceptive, since curves (especially gentle ones) as well as straight lines can be stitched with this technique.

1. Set stitch length for six to ten stitches per inch and attach walking foot to sewing machine.

2. Determine which section of quilt will have longest continuous quilting line, oftentimes area from center top to center bottom. Roll up and secure each edge of quilt to help reduce the bulk, keeping fabrics smooth. Smaller projects may not need to be rolled.
3. Begin stitching on longest quilting line, using very short stitches for the first $1/4$" to "lock" quilting. Stitch across project, using one hand on each side of walking foot to slightly spread fabric and to guide fabric through machine. Lock stitches at end of quilting line.
4. Continue machine quilting, stitching longer quilting lines first to stabilize quilt before moving on to other areas.

Free-Motion Quilting

Free-motion quilting may be free form or may follow a marked pattern.

1. Attach darning foot to sewing machine and lower or cover feed dogs.
2. Position quilt under darning foot; lower foot. Holding top thread, take a stitch and pull bobbin thread to top of quilt. To "lock" beginning of quilting line, hold top and bobbin threads while making three to five stitches in place.
3. Use one hand on each side of darning foot to slightly spread fabric and to move fabric through the machine. Even stitch length is achieved by using smooth, flowing hand motion and steady machine speed. Slow machine speed and fast hand movement will create long stitches. Fast machine speed and slow hand movement will create short stitches. Move quilt sideways, back and forth, in a circular motion, or in a random motion to create desired designs; do not rotate quilt. Lock stitches at end of each quilting line.

MAKING A HANGING SLEEVE

Attaching a hanging sleeve to back of wall hanging or quilt before the binding is added allows project to be displayed on wall.

1. Measure width of quilt top edge and subtract 1". Cut piece of fabric 7"w by determined measurement.
2. Press short edges of fabric piece $1/4$" to wrong side; press edges $1/4$" to wrong side again and machine stitch in place.
3. Matching wrong sides, fold piece in half lengthwise to form tube.
4. Follow project instructions to sew binding to quilt top and to trim backing and batting. Before Blindstitching binding to backing, match raw edges and stitch hanging sleeve to center top edge on back of quilt.
5. Finish binding quilt, treating hanging sleeve as part of backing.
6. Blindstitch bottom of hanging sleeve to backing, taking care not to stitch through to front of quilt.
7. Insert dowel or slat into hanging sleeve.

BINDING

Making Straight-Grain Binding

1. Using a diagonal seam, sew bindng strips together end-to-end.
2. Matching wrong sides and raw edges, press strip(s) in half lengthwise to complete binding.

Attaching Binding With Mitered Corners

1. Matching wrong sides and raw edges, press strip(s) in half lengthwise to complete binding.
2. Beginning with one end near center on bottom edge of quilt, lay binding around quilt to make sure that seams in binding will not end up at a corner. Adjust placement if necessary. Matching raw edges of binding to raw edge of quilt top, pin binding to right side of quilt along one edge.

3. When you reach first corner, mark $1/4$" from corner of quilt top (**Fig. 22**).

Fig. 22

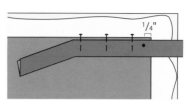

4. Beginning approximately 10" from end of binding and using $1/4$" seam allowance, sew binding to quilt, backstitching at beginning of stitching and at mark (**Fig. 23**). Lift needle out of fabric and clip thread.

Fig. 23

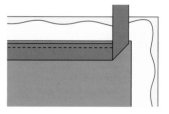

5. Fold binding as shown in **Figs. 24-25** and pin binding to adjacent side, matching raw edges. When you've reached the next corner, mark $1/4$" from edge of quilt top.

Fig. 24

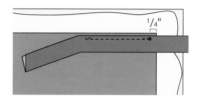

Fig. 25

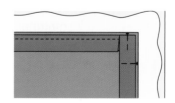

6. Backstitching at edge of quilt top, sew pinned binding to quilt (**Fig. 26**); backstitch at the next mark. Lift needle out of fabric and clip thread.

Fig. 26

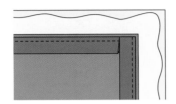

7. Continue sewing binding to quilt, stopping approximately 10" from starting point (**Fig. 27**).

Fig. 27

8. Bring beginning and end of binding to center of opening and fold each end back, leaving a ¹⁄₄" space between folds (**Fig. 28**). Finger press folds.

Fig. 28

9. Unfold ends of binding and draw a line across wrong side in finger-pressed crease. Draw a line through the lengthwise pressed fold of binding at the same spot to create a cross mark. With edge of ruler at cross mark, line up 45° angle marking on ruler with one long side of binding. Draw a diagonal line from edge to edge. Repeat on remaining end, making sure that the two diagonal lines are angled the same way (**Fig. 29**).

Fig. 29

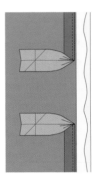

10. Matching right sides and diagonal lines, pin binding ends together at right angles (**Fig. 30**).

Fig. 30

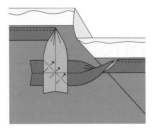

11. Machine stitch along diagonal line (**Fig. 31**), removing pins as you stitch.

Fig. 31

12. Lay binding against quilt to double check that it is correct length.

13. Trim binding ends, leaving $1/4$" seam allowance; press seam open. Stitch binding to quilt.

14. If using $2^1/2$"w binding (finished size $1/2$"), trim backing and batting a scant $1/4$" larger than quilt top so that batting and backing will fill the binding when it is folded over to quilt backing. If using narrower binding, trim backing and batting even with edges of quilt top.

15. On one edge of quilt, fold binding over to quilt backing and pin pressed edge in place, covering stitching line (**Fig. 32**). On adjacent side, fold binding over, forming a mitered corner (**Fig. 33**). Repeat to pin remainder of binding in place.

Fig. 32 **Fig. 33**

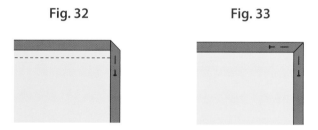

16. Blindstitch binding to backing, taking care not to stitch through to front of quilt.

MAKING A CONTINUOUS BIAS STRIP

1. Cut Bias Square in half diagonally to make 2 triangles. With right sides together and using a $1/4$" seam allowance, sew triangles together (**Fig. 34**). Press seam allowance open.

Fig. 34

2. On the wrong side of the fabric, draw lines $1^1/2$" apart. Cut off any fabric less than this width (**Fig. 35**).

Fig. 35

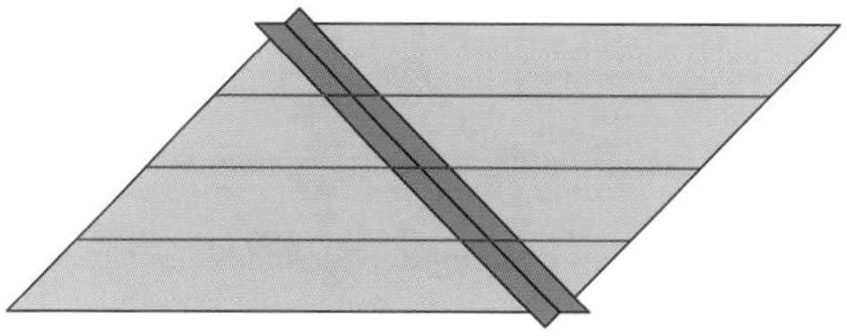

3. With right sides inside, bring short edges together to make a tube; match raw edges so that the first drawn line of the top section meets the second drawn line of the bottom section (**Fig. 36**).

Fig. 36

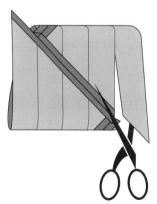

4. Being sure the drawn lines match exactly, pin the edges together. Using a $1/4$" seam allowance, sew edges together. Press seam allowance open.

5. To cut a continuous strip, begin cutting along first drawn line (**Fig. 37**). Continue cutting along drawn line around tube. Trim ends of bias strip square.

Fig. 37

Metric Conversion Chart

Inches x 2.54 = centimeters (cm)
Inches x 25.4 = millimeters (mm)
Inches x .0254 = meters (m)

Yards x .9144 = meters (m)
Yards x 91.44 = centimeters (cm)
Centimeters x .3937 = inches (")
Meters x 1.0936 = yards (yd)

Standard Equivalents

1/8"	3.2 mm	0.32 cm	1/8 yard	11.43 cm	0.11 m
1/4"	6.35 mm	0.635 cm	1/4 yard	22.86 cm	0.23 m
3/8"	9.5 mm	0.95 cm	3/8 yard	34.29 cm	0.34 m
1/2"	12.7 mm	1.27 cm	1/2 yard	45.72 cm	0.46 m
5/8"	15.9 mm	1.59 cm	5/8 yard	57.15 cm	0.57 m
3/4"	19.1 mm	1.91 cm	3/4 yard	68.58 cm	0.69 m
7/8"	22.2 mm	2.22 cm	7/8 yard	80 cm	0.8 m
1"	25.4 mm	2.54 cm	1 yard	91.44 cm	0.91 m

Glory Days

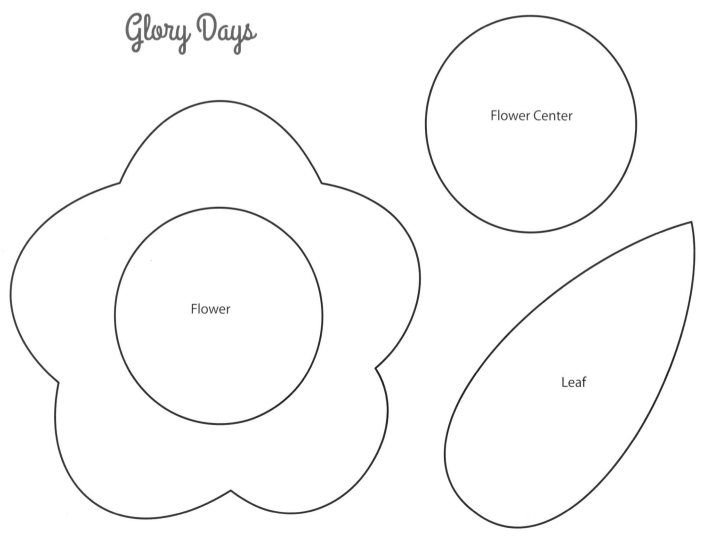

Flower Center

Flower

Leaf

Star of The Old West

To trace a complete pattern onto template plastic, trace half pattern. Flip template plastic and align fold line on pattern with drawn fold line on template plastic, trace remaining half pattern

To trace a complete pattern onto fusible web, trace half pattern. With paper side out fold the web in half along fold line and trace along previously drawn lines.

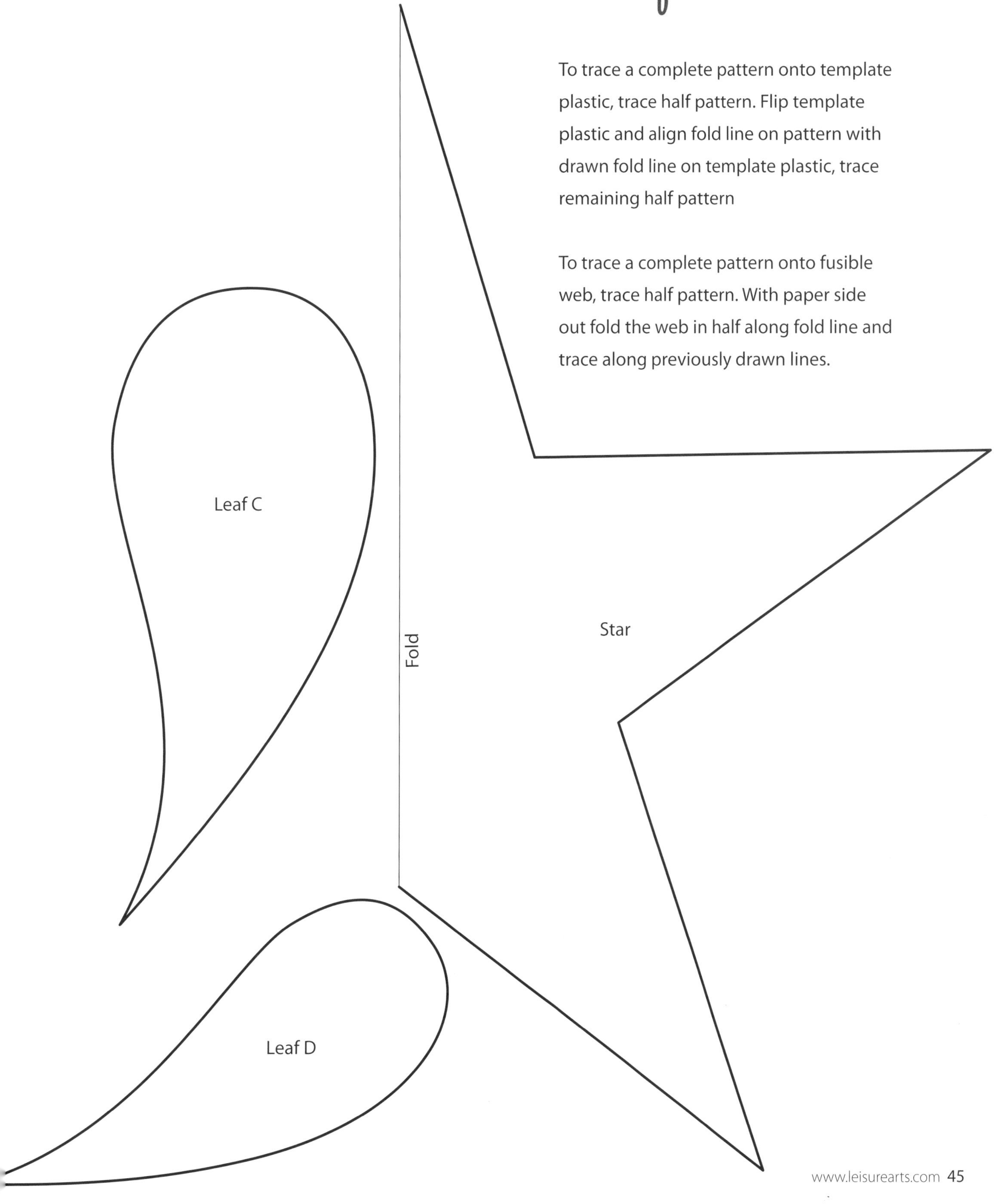

Leaf C

Fold

Star

Leaf D

To trace a complete pattern onto template plastic, trace half pattern. Flip template plastic and align fold line on pattern with drawn fold line on template plastic, trace remaining half pattern

To trace a complete pattern onto fusible web, trace half pattern. With paper side out fold the web in half along fold line and trace along previously drawn lines.

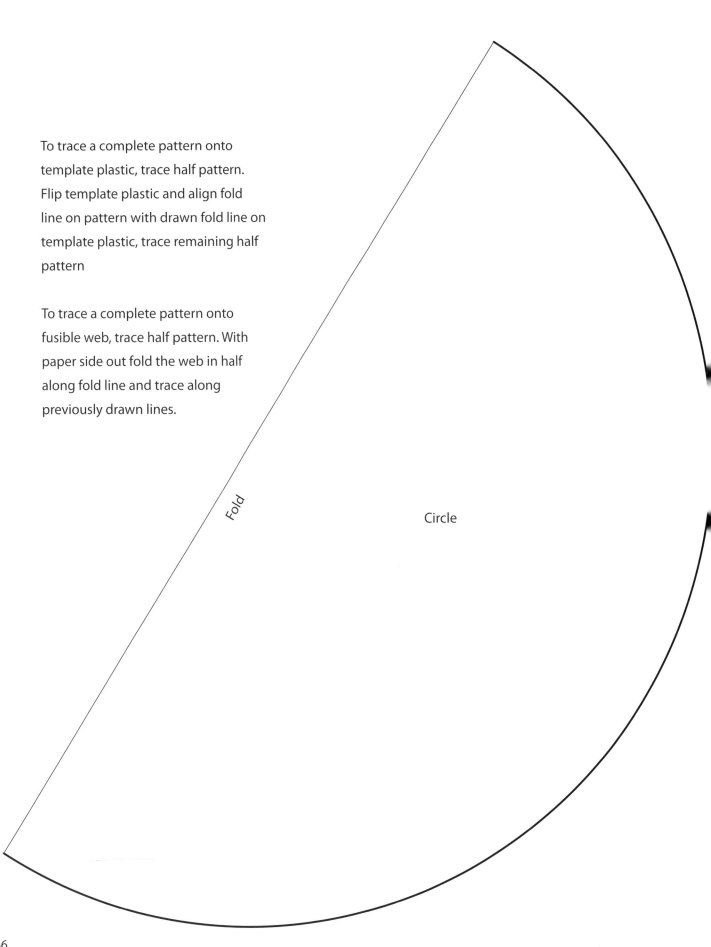

Fold

Circle

Meet Nancy Rink

Passionate about fabrics of many styles, Nancy Rink is a quilter, designer, and dye artist who enjoys combining piecing and appliqué. "For me," she says, "nothing tops off a pieced quilt like a little bit of appliqué."

Admired for their exquisite stitching and color flow, her eclectic designs have won numerous national and international awards.

Nancy took the plunge as a full-time quilting professional after 23 years of teaching junior high and high school English. Nowadays, customers can shop for her fabric and kits and find her working at the Nancy Rink Designs studio in Bakersfield, California. As a licensed designer for Marcus Fabrics, she creates two to three fabric collections per year and the patterns to accompany them. She also develops block of the month programs for Marcus, some of which have included the popular Amish With a Twist programs.

Nancy has had quilts published in numerous quilting magazines and in three earlier Leisure Arts books (*Quilts That Honor Tradition* #6698, *City Blocks* #5735, and *Quilts to Warm Today's Home* #5736). She also is co-author (with her husband, Oliver) of *Away From Home: Quilts Inspired by the Lowell Factory Girls* and *El Camino Real: Quilts Inspired by Early California History*.

For more information, shopping, and a gallery of some of Nancy's award winning quilts, visit her website, nancyrinkdesigns.com, and her Facebook page.

Production Team: Technical Editor – Jean Lewis; Associate Editor – Lisa Lancaster; Editorial Writer – Susan Frantz Wiles; Senior Graphic Artist – Lora Puls; Graphic Artist – Kytanna McFarlin; Photography Stylists – Lori Wenger; Photographer - Jason Masters

We have made every effort to ensure that these instructions are accurate and complete. We cannot, however, be responsible for human error, typographical mistakes, or variations in individual work.